# STEEL BEAMS & IRON MEN

# STEEL BEAMS & IRON MEN

# BY MIKE CHERRY

FOUR WINDS PRESS

NEW YORK

PHOTO CREDITS

Ray Ellis/Photo Researchers, Inc., 5, 21, 40, 47, 53
Margot Granitsas/Photo Researchers, Inc., 33
Lewis W. Hine/International Museum of Photography
at the George Eastman House, iii, 2, 9, 14, 15, 58, 83
George E. Jones III/Photo Researchers, Inc., 56
Robert Mottar/Chase Manhattan Bank, 12, 24, 28, 36,
43, 48, 63, 69, 74, 78, 87

Library of Congress Cataloging in Publication Data
Cherry, Mike [date].
Steel beams and iron men.
Summary: An ironworker describes his experiences
erecting steel frames of large structures such as
skyscrapers and industrial plants in New York City
and a California desert.
1. Iron and steel workers — United States — Juvenile
literature.    2. Building trades — United States —
Juvenile literature.    [1. Iron and steel workers.
2. Building, Iron and steel]    I. Title.
HD8039.I52U527    691'.7'02373    80-66246
ISBN 0-590-07591-8
Published by Four Winds Press
A division of Scholastic, Inc., New York, N.Y.
Copyright © 1980 by Mike Cherry
All rights reserved
Printed in the United States of America
Library of Congress Catalog Card Number: 80-66246
Book design by Kathleen Westray
1  2  3  4  5  84  83  82  81  80

For LARRY and DENNY and MATTY
and a whole bunch of other old friends

"How much you figure we got up there, Jiggs?" I asked.

"Oh, I dunno," he said, working with his little finger at some wax in his ear, "sixteen, eighteen t'ousand tons, I guess."

We all nodded in reflection. It wasn't exactly an impressive figure, but it did have a certain ring to it.

"I've spent whole years in the sticks without hangin' that much iron," said Patrick.

"Well," Jiggs offered, "it's bigger'n a breadbox."

—FROM AN EARLIER WORK
OF THE AUTHOR'S

# INTRODUCTION

T H E R E are some jobs that are dull and that can't be any other way no matter how you slice it. And sometimes, by mistake or because they weren't looking, people wind up in them. I mean, nobody ever grew up actually *planning* to be a file clerk or a night watchman, did he? Not that I'm knocking either clerks or watchmen, understand; both are honorable occupations. But they've got to be dull.

And there are some jobs that go, for me at least, too far in the other direction: underwater demolition work, driving high-explosives trucks, getting shot out of cannons at circuses. I like a little excitement, but I can't remember ever being out-front suicidal.

And there are some jobs that have a nice balance built in, with a little routine activity—which is good because it's hard on the heart to

go around wound up *all* the time—and a little excitement—because it's good for the ego and provides a rewarding sense of involvement.

I didn't find that last kind until I was thirty-five, which says, I guess, that I was pretty slow to realize that my life was dull. For most of it I'd been a schoolteacher, which I'd enjoyed but which is a lot closer to a file clerk than to a human cannonball. When I finally did realize it I quit my job, joined three other people in the purchase of a small sailboat, and set out around the world. I wasn't sure if it was the right thing to do, but I knew it was time to do *something*. It turned out, though, to be a mighty short cruise. We left Tom's River, New Jersey, one fine September morning, and lost a violent argument to a hurricane off Cape Hatteras (the northeastern tip of North Carolina, famous for its vicious weather) the day after Thanksgiving. No one was hurt, but the boat was destroyed, and we were financially wiped out.

I then took a job as a mill hand and was trying damned hard to put together enough bucks to quit when an acquaintance told me he could get me a job as an ironworker. I had only the foggiest kind of notion about what an ironworker was, but I accepted as fast as I could. The mill work was driving me bananas with its monotony, and it seemed only logical to grab at any opportunity for a change.

And within a few days I knew that, however casual the search had been, I had found something that was going to be important to me.

A connector, sent aloft to correct a mechanical problem, signals to his gang from the top of the derrick, the "spider."

Ironworkers are the men who erect the steel frames that support most tall buildings, industrial plants, conventional and nuclear power installations, bridges, radio and television transmission towers, and the giant dish antennas of radiotelescopes. If a structure has steel in it, ironworkers helped build it.

To be honest, some of the work *is* dull, requiring of the worker only that he be physically strong. And some of it is dangerous as hell, requiring strength, courage, skill, experience, and intelligence. That's the balance I spoke of earlier. And all of it has an important inherent satisfaction: *making* something. Most of the human race seems to take pleasure in making things, yet few jobs provide that satisfaction in any direct sense. Along with a few other fortunate folk, though, the construction worker doesn't have to deal in abstractions. His product is right there in front of him, growing day by day. Nor is it cuckoo clocks or porcelain dolls, either. It might be a skyscraper five hundred or a thousand feet high with a hundred thousand tons of steel in it, or a radiotelescope antenna made of beams so delicate that when completed it looks like a flower three hundred feet across. He might construct a suspension bridge, such as the Verrazano Narrows Bridge at the mouth of New York harbor, which is so big that its roadbed is more than twenty feet higher in winter, when the steel shrinks in the cold, than in summer, when it expands in the heat.

For some kinds of people, then, construction work can be a pretty good thing. Yes, some of it is dull, but much of it is exciting, and all of

A connector moving cautiously along an extremely narrow piece.

it is hazardous enough to keep the adrenalin flowing and the nerves tingling, and in the end it provides an ego trip of a morally desirable sort: the pride a person is allowed to take in having come to terms with fear.

And I'd be lying if I didn't admit that it's a hell of a pleasure to be able to walk in the shadows of skyscrapers in a number of cities, and some refineries here and there, and a pretty fair-sized chemical plant in the Mojave desert and be able to look up and say, "By God, a piece of that is *mine.*"

# WHO ARE ALL THOSE PEOPLE UP THERE?

MOST people seem to think that ironworkers are all, or nearly all, Indians. It isn't so. There *are* Indians, of course (they make up perhaps 5 to 10 percent of the total work force, though a much higher percentage in the Northeast), but there are also Hispanics, blacks, and several varieties of whites: Irish Catholics, southern Protestants, Newfoundlers, Midwesterners of Swedish and Norwegian ancestry, and so on. If they share a common heritage it is probably one of economic disenfranchisement. That is, at some point in the past each group was poor, and, without the tool of higher education, they had no escape route into the middle class except through skilled physical labor. That such labor was dangerous was irrelevant.

The first Indians to become ironworkers did so when a cantilever bridge was to be erected across the St. Lawrence River near Montreal, in 1886. Part of the project passed through a section of the Caughnawaga reservation, and to gain permission to go through it the builders agreed to hire many of the local Indians. When the project was completed, many of them, now equipped with a skill and accustomed to earning good cash wages, stayed with the trade, following it to Toronto, Buffalo, New York, and other Northeastern cities.

They're good at it, but there are no statistics to support the common white-collar belief that Indians have some extraordinary sense of balance. There are no figures showing that they fall less frequently than any other group. There probably *is* something to the notion that as a group they are particularly well suited to a trade that requires skill, daring, and courage: these are qualities much admired and respected among all American Indian tribes.

Newfoundland, a large island off the eastern coast of Canada, supports itself principally through its fishing industry. There is little manufacturing, and consequently not much opportunity for a young man to turn a "cash crop." To earn cash many of its young people, starting in the late 1920s and continuing on to today, moved to the mainland. The harsh traditions of the sea seem to have prepared these "Newfies" very well for the rough outdoor life of the ironworker. If there's any truth in the ethnic generalizations related to ironworkers, it is that the Newfies complain less about the cold of winter than do the rest of us.

I get the shivers every time I think of a wiry little man named

On the weight ball.

Eddie. He came to work an hour or more early every morning and changed into his work clothes before the shanty's propane heaters had taken the least chill off the air. Then he climbed stairs and ladders to the top of the job (the partial-lift elevators don't run until it's time to go to work) and sat on the January iron, five hundred feet high, facing the dawn wind, and while waiting for the rest of the gang to show up —he drank a couple of ice-cold beers.

One thing about the Newfies, though: they like fish tails. They cook them atop the wire screens of the charcoal braziers that we keep fired up in winter to warm our hands. To be able to work downwind of one of these operations requires a totally dead nose.

The Irish began immigrating to America during the potato famine of the 1860s. Most of them had been farmers, and had little schooling. They were widely looked down upon, but they were industrious, and they took what work they could find, performing it well. Many became cops or firemen, and many went into the construction trades and became ironworkers. Their sons were encouraged to go to school to be able to become "better" than their fathers, but many also became ironworkers. (Some became priests, and I have one friend who became *both*.)

In any event, while it's true that in the past the less-educated poor provided society with the bulk of its blue-collar workers, it's also true that today you will find many construction workers whose considerable education would have allowed them employment in other fields had they so chosen. They did not. Therefore there must be some satisfaction to be found in the work itself.

# AND WHAT IN HELL ARE THEY DOING UP THERE?

IRONWORKERS, despite their name, put together structures made of steel. They belong to a union whose official name is The International Association of Bridge, Structural, and Ornamental Ironworkers, but they work with steel. They are not the men who smelt the ore or who roll out the bars into sheets and beams or who cut and shape the metal to dimensions determined by architects and engineers. Ironworkers are the men who bolt and rivet and weld these finished pieces together, wrestling and levering and pounding and shoving the structural components of *anything* made of steel into place.

In the late nineteenth and early twentieth centuries they *did* work with iron: the few "large" buildings erected in those days had external supporting walls of masonry (concrete and brickwork), and their

floors rested upon massive beams of cast iron that stretched from wall to opposite wall. In setting these beams into place they became known as "ironworkers." By today's standards the buildings they put up were pretty strange looking. Cast iron is heavy as all get out, and the amount of masonry required to support beams made of it is hard to believe: the Monadnock Building in Chicago, completed in 1908 and at that time the nation's leading "skyscraper" at something on the order of 220 feet high, had walls that were at ground level *sixteen feet thick.* Entering it must have felt like going through a tunnel.

But then economical processes for producing steel were developed, and the day of cast iron—a heavy, thick, clumsy material that can be formed only when molten and that cannot be bent, welded, stretched, shaved, or cut—was over. With steel, a far lighter material that is ductile, bendable, resilient, easily weldable and cutable, the modern city—essentially a vertical phenomenon—began to take shape.

In New York, an ideal site for such a city because of the solidity of the rock beneath it, great skyscrapers began going up one after the other: the Woolworth Tower, the Chrysler Building, the Empire State Building. On all of these the placing, connecting, riveting, bolting, and welding of the steel was done by ironworkers. Today the high-strength bolt has rendered the rivet obsolete (except in certain kinds of bridge building) and the engines used to power the derricks and cranes that hoist the columns and beams into place are a little more sophisticated; but the fundamental techniques of building megastruc-

Driving in a pin to align the holes.

*(opposite)* **Riveting a corner joint.**
"Shaking out." **Sorting the iron on the plank floor.**

tures remain largely as they were at the beginning. In fact, if you were to paint jeans and sweatshirts over the coveralls and ties of those men in photographs of buildings under construction in the thirties, it would be very hard to be sure that you weren't looking at shots of buildings being erected today.

Of course the contemporary ironworker also labors on structures his grandfather (or even father) never heard of: missile silos and giant antennas, space-probe launch cages, atomic power plants, microwave-relay towers, and giant offshore oil rigs. Yet despite the development of these new *kinds* of structures, the skills employed in erecting them have not been that much altered: the nerve, strength, and agility needed to bolt up tiny beams atop a launch tower are the same as were needed to do it on the Chrysler Building. The knowledge how best to "walk" a ten-ton header into place between two twenty-ton columns on an atomic power plant was first acquired on the skyscrapers that went up fifty years ago, and has been handed down through three generations of ironworkers.

It may be because of an unconscious sense of that continuity that ironworkers insist upon being called by their now-misleading name. In any case there are 177,000 of them in this country, and every one of them will get sore at you if you call them "steelworkers." They're *iron*workers, and damned proud of it.

# JUST WHAT DO THESE GUYS DO?

WELL, the first question is, "Which guys?" There are seventeen separate major construction trade unions, and over fifty-five sub-trades. Each specializes in a certain kind of work, and because of the natural desire of any man to protect his laboriously acquired skills from being imitated by a klutz, these unions have developed contracts that prevent outsiders from performing their work. An ironworker may not install glass. A glazier (who *does* install glass) may not string electrical cables. An electrician may not bolt a piece of iron into place. . . .

In very general terms, this is how a building goes up: one trade digs a hole in the ground; another pours concrete walls around its perimeter and sinks *piers* (subterranean columns) deep into the earth, capping them with concrete pads (squares of concrete that may be as much as two feet thick and six feet on a side); the ironworkers come in and, with cranes, place *billet plates* atop the pads. Billet plates are steel slabs that may vary, depending upon the size of the structure that will rest on them, from three to seven inches in thickness and from two to five feet on a side. From that point on the building goes up just like a giant erector set.

With a few oddball exceptions, steel buildings are essentially boxes made of vertical and horizontal steel sticks. Vertical pieces are called *columns.* Horizontal pieces that connect one column to another are called *headers.* Pieces that run from one header to the next are called *beams. Outside* headers, of course, are those pieces that connect the columns on the perimeter of a building. Since they bear more weight—the building walls—they are generally larger than the *inside* headers.

When the cranes have set the first three or four floors of the building, the derricks are brought in and stood in place by the cranes, which then leave. Derricks are those two-piece towers (one fixed, one movable) that you see atop budding buildings. They are used to pick up iron from trucks in the street and to set the pieces in place on succeeding floors. Derricks rise with the building. One of the masts is used to hoist the other into the next elevation and anchored. Once in place, that mast is used to raise the first.

The ironworkers who work the derricks form a group called the *raising gang.* A raising gang consists of six men and a *pusher,* or

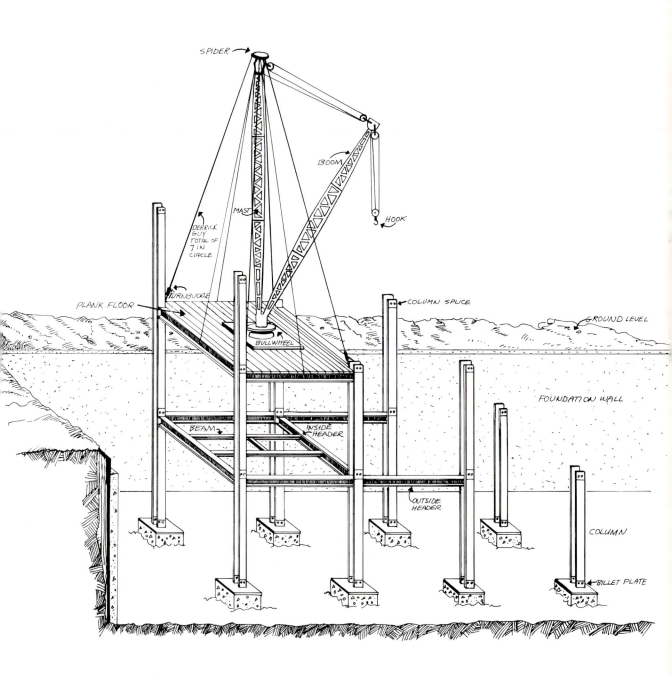

SPIDER

BOOM

HOOK

MAST

DERRICK
GUY
TOTAL OF
7 IN
CIRCLE

COLUMN SPLICE

GROUND LEVEL

TURNBUCKLE

PLANK FLOOR

BULLWHEEL

FOUNDATION WALL

BEAM

INSIDE
HEADER

OUTSIDE
HEADER

COLUMN

BILLET PLATE

boss. The *hooker-on* is the man responsible for placing wire cables, called chokers, around the iron pieces to be set. While he makes a piece ready, the *tagline man* attaches a rope to one end of it, which he will use to steer the piece as it ascends. When the piece is ready, the *bell man* punches a button on a box he wears around his neck. By means of this box he is electrically connected to the engineer who, from far below and out of sight, operates the machinery that controls the cables which cause the derrick to raise or lower its load or to tip its *boom*—the movable mast—in or out. At the foot of the derrick is a seat on which the *bullwheel man* sits. By turning a large wheel, he controls the lateral movement of the derrick. Thus, between *booming up* (or down) and rotating the derrick laterally, a load can be placed anywhere in the area.

Once the first columns have been set, two *connectors* shinny up them and, hanging on any way they can, await the arrival of the first header. When it is steered within reach by the tagline man, they grab it and cut the tagline loose. The piece is now their responsibility. Giving hand signal instructions to the bell man and the bullwheel man, the connectors wrestle the header into place, called *home*. They use their *spud wrenches* (long open-end wrenches with tapered handles) to align the holes in the column with those in the header, drop a couple of bolts into adjacent holes, and run up the nuts. Then one of them trots out to the center of the piece and, when the bell man lowers the hook until the strain is released, cuts the choker loose. Then the process starts all over again.

Making up a header. The man on the left could use a new bolt bag.

When all the iron in one section has been set, the *bolter-ups* come along. The connectors place only enough bolts to keep the iron from falling down; the bolter-ups are responsible for placing the full complement—which on a large *point,* or intersection, could be as many as a hundred. At certain connections—principally where the top of one column is joined to the bottom of the next—welding is also called for; the welders arrive with their hoods and their buckets of welding rods and make themselves comfortable, for it may take up to two hours to weld a single large seam.

As the sections of new iron are completed the *plank gang* begins laying out a temporary floor. Somewhere, several stories below the derrick, is another plank gang taking up a lower floor. They bundle the planks at the building's edge so the derrick will be able to reach over the side and down to pick the boards up for later use.

When all the iron is set the derrick is *jumped,* and all the while this is going on there are other men performing other tasks: the *plumbing-up gang,* using heavy cables and turnbuckles, pulls the columns this way and that until they are vertical. Engineers come along behind them with their transits, and argue with the plumber-ups about whether they've gotten it right. Apprentices carry buckets of bolts to the bolter-ups. The *detail gang* installs by hand small pieces of iron that the raising squad does not bother with. (Why tie up an expensive piece of machinery and seven men for a six-foot-long beam that two men can hoist by themselves?) Gofers go for coffee. And everywhere there are pushers and supers and other sorts of bosses.

All of these men are ironworkers. On a big job, such as the McGraw-Hill Building in New York City, there might be as many as a hundred ironworkers at any one time. Yet once the building is a few stories high, the men from the other trades descend on the job in earnest, installing elevators, pouring concrete, putting in plumbing, wiring, glass, marble, siding, flooring, air conditioners, and everything else that goes into the marvelously complicated vertical city that a skyscraper really is. At the height of construction of the Chrysler Tower, there were five thousand men at work. But the ironworkers, up on the top, see little of the confusion all this activity causes. Where they are, no one else can be, because it isn't there until they put it there.

When the highest elevation is reached, a ceremony and a party are held. The placing of the highest column is witnessed by a variety of officials, each one looking sillier than the next in white hard hats and immaculate suits, striking poses with sledge hammers at the base of the column while pictures are shot for the newspapers.

An American flag is attached to the top of the highest column, in the East. In the West, they send an evergreen tree up. No one seems to know how either custom got started, but in any case, when the speeches and picture taking are over, the "topping out" party begins.

Topping out parties are rather bittersweet affairs. Sometimes the contractor will rent an entire cocktail lounge and serve the men good food and drink; sometimes he'll simply set up some tables on a lower floor and put out sandwiches and kegs of beer. (In better economic

times men have been known to refuse to work for companies with poor party records.) I said bittersweet because while the end of a job means the onset of anxiety about what the next one will be, there is also that sense of accomplishment that rises when you can look up into the sky and see the whole damn thing finished.

It's an illusion, of course: the building is *not* finished. There is still some iron to set; there may be revisions made on several floors; there are plumbing-up cables to be taken out; there are the derricks to take down, materials to be hauled off. It might be six or eight more weeks before the ironworkers' part of the job is actually over; and the other trades, still working their way to the top, might be another six months in wrapping up.

But for the raising gang, the end is at hand. Many of them will quit that very day, because the challenge is gone. They want to be off to the next one.

A three-derrick job nears completion.

# WHY WOULD ANYBODY IN HIS RIGHT MIND DO THIS FOR A LIVING?

I SUPPOSE everybody has a certain amount of fear as he approaches any new job—of the boss, or of being unable to discharge his obligations because of insufficient training or some previously undiscovered personal inadequacy—a fear of failure in general. But an ironworker faces, on top of these things, so to speak, the fear of heights. Not *every* ironworker, but certainly most.

The two times I've been most scared were the very first time I went up on a job, and the first time I went looking for work in New York. The odd thing about that is that in neither case was there really anything to be afraid of.

My first job was on a little platform off the side of a building, twenty-three stories up. I didn't have to do anything difficult, and the only way I could have fallen would have been to suffer an attack of vertigo, black out, and collapse over the edge. I was, nevertheless, frightened. It was clear, though, that no one around me was frightened, and I was damned if I was going to let them see that I was. The day passed, somehow, and after it a very long night of self-examination, lying in bed wondering why I had entered into such an obviously crazy trade. But the next morning I went to work and didn't have as much trouble handling the fear as I had had on the first day. I assumed the worst was over. Once I realized I could handle the height I began to be rather proud of myself.

Unjustifiably, it turned out. When work slowed in the smaller towns, word began going around that there were still jobs in New York. By then I'd acquired some experience and a little skill, and I told my wife I was going to see if I could get something in the city. I drove into Manhattan so that I could cruise down the spine of the city and see what was being erected. By the time I got to lower Broadway I was shaking: there were skyscrapers going up all over the place, and my God, they were *big.* The twenty-three-story building that I had thought of as the proving ground of my courage suddenly seemed like an outhouse.

The response that ironworkers customarily give to laymen who ask about the effect of great height upon them—"After the first three floors it makes no difference; any fall over thirty feet is odds-on to kill you"—suddenly seemed the cheapest sort of baloney. I repeated it to myself several times, but it didn't help. I pulled the car to the curb

beneath a seventy-two-story monster, leaned out the window, and stared up at the top. There were men walking around up there. Microscopic at a distance of some 900 feet, but recognizable men—on eight- or ten-inch beams, trotting along with their heavy tools and carrying heavy materials.

I panicked, pulled away from the curb, and drove home. When my wife asked what had happened in the city, I told her that there was no work, that the hiring hall was full of men waiting for jobs.

And in bed that night I wasn't very proud of myself, having caught myself out a liar and a coward. There was nothing to do but go down to New York again the next day, which I did. I was sent right to work, and before the week was out had learned tall structures are more frightening to look up at than down from. Since that time I've been dangled by one arm from a rope hanging from a beam that swung out over Sixth Avenue when it shouldn't have, been knocked off a derrick by its bull wheel in a freakish accident that broke my back, been nearly knocked from more than a dozen columns when headers were slammed into them too hard, been thrown into the water from a bridge (low, thank goodness) we were dismantling when the burner at the other end cut completely through its anchor without checking to see if I was still on the piece. (Mind you, these things happen to *all* ironworkers.) But I really don't recall ever again being as plain scared as I was that first day in New York.

In time I learned that many of the men I was working with had once had second thoughts. I met seasoned hands like Denny Con-

Checking to see what's happening below.

nolly, who saw nothing shameful in admitting to early fear. "My father was an ironworker," Denny told me over a beer one night, "and my uncles were, too. I came home from school one summer—I was eighteen and studying to be a priest—and pointed out to my family that the next school year would be a lot easier on us all if I could earn some serious summer money. So my father got me a permit to go ironworking, which my mother didn't like one bit. She didn't think construction work was the right thing for me to be doing during my vacation. But my dad told her that as a beginner I'd be working on the ground and wouldn't be in any danger. I went off to work the next day, happy as a pig in clover to be making good money, and not the least bit worried, because I, too, had believed the line he'd given her.

"Then at eight o'clock the whistle went off and the pusher looked at me and said, 'You there, boy Connolly! Report to Kenny. He's wearin' a blue hat with a stripe.' I looked all around but I didn't see anybody in a blue hat, so I went back to the pusher and said, 'Where is he?' and he said, 'On top, dummy; where'd you *expect* him to be?' I looked up at the top and just about died. The job was up twenty, maybe twenty-two floors, and when I finally got there I looked through the gaps between the planks and I didn't much like what I saw. I think I went to the crapper about two dozen times that day. The old man had suckered us both; he'd known perfectly well I'd be sent up top. They put me to carrying bolts, and I got through the day okay, but the Porta-potty took a beating."

Still, my favorite story about early fear of heights is told by Tom

Leary. Tom is a gigantic man shaped like a carrot: great, beamy shoulders, a middle-sized torso, and tapering legs. He's about the same color as a carrot, too, with orange hair and unusually fair skin covered with freckles from head to toe. Tom is a man capable of climbing six floors of ladders while carrying a two-hundred-pound keg of bolts. "Fellow I knew from Sheepshead Bay got me my first job," he told me, "which was just coming out of the hole." (Skyscrapers have basements that are often five or six floors deep. The excavation into which these subfloors are placed is literally a hole, and a falling man would land in it. In common usage, however, nearly *any* fall is called "going into the hole," whether the worker tumbles down an elevator shaft or over the side all the way to the ground or goes only two stories to a completed floor. There's a bit of macho to be found here, though, since a fall of less than two floors qualifies only as "taking a flop.")

"The iron was right at street level, so it didn't look like much of anything until you got right up on it," Tom said. "Then you could see that even though it wasn't much of a hole—two floors—you'd get banged up if you went in. The pusher was going to put me to work on the far side of the building, so he goes straight at the hole and starts walking across this big header, saying, 'Follow me, kid.' I take a look at what he's walking on and say to myself, what is this guy, nuts? Now, it's a big piece, maybe a sixteen-incher, but at the time it looks to me like a tightrope. How, I think, do I do this? The man is obviously crazy. But he's not aware that I'm just standing there; he's just strolling on across. I'm trying to figure out how to go at this damned ribbon, looking around for *any* kind of answer, when I see that there's a ladder right beside the header that goes down to the bottom of the hole. So I quick skinny down it, run across the hole, find a ladder on the other side, shoot up it as fast as I can, and meet him just as he's stepping off the thing onto the ground. I'm pretty pleased with myself, but he gives me a long, sad look and says, 'My boy, I don't think you're gonna make it.' ''

But he did. He stuck with it, and in time became quite a respected connector. And when I went to an alteration job (after a flop and a four-month recuperation period) that he was already on, a job that required carrying heavy tools across an eighty-foot span of a five-inch-wide beam ninety feet up—with nothing at all to grab hold of in the event of a stumble—he went on over with his load, came back and grabbed mine from me, and said, "You ain't been on open iron in a long time; I'll carry the tools; you take it easy till you get your legs back."

I appreciated it, but it wasn't an act of charity, exactly, nor of condescension, either. We all try to help a man who's out of shape or practice (or, as in my case, both), or who's just recovering from an injury. The work is tough enough even when you've got your act together, and a sensible man accepts whatever help he's offered.

I didn't fall on that job, and after a few days back at work I was again comfortable on the iron. But the fact that a man successfully conquers his fear of falling—or that, for whatever reason, he's never

Coming out of the hole.

had one—is no guarantee that he *won't* fall. On the contrary, complacency leads to carelessness, and carelessness is more dangerous than high winds and narrow beams. Even the most experienced men regularly caution one another with the oldest adage in the trade: One hand for yourself; one hand for the job.

# ON ACROPHOBIA

ACCORDING to a psychologist named Leonard Elkun, a fear of heights—acrophobia—is a fear of self: a person develops an aversion to high or exposed places because a part of him realizes that if he were to take one more step, his problem would be settled. Since the rest of him would rather have the problems than croak, he becomes suddenly dizzy and gets quickly away from the edge. I have no way of knowing whether this is accurate (though it sounds good), but it doesn't matter much, because when you've got it you've got it, and if you mean to be an ironworker, you had better get over it.

Larry Miller, who's been my partner on jobs in New York and New Jersey and California, pretty much said the same thing—without ever having seen that study on acrophobia, of course. We were having

coffee while sitting on an outside header five hundred feet above Sixth Avenue, enjoying the short break in the middle of a particularly hard morning, when he remarked, "You know, if I was to give my ass a teeny wiggle I wouldn't have to pay the rent anymore." We were dangling our legs and looking between them at the scurrying bugs below that were really people and cars. Somebody else on the beam said, "Aw, shut up." Larry shrugged and answered, "I never said I was *going* to, or even that I *wanted* to; I was just pointing out that I *could*."

Which, of course, is the key to the whole thing: you *could* but you don't. I've seen men fall, but I've never seen one *jump*.

# FAST ENOUGH TO GET THERE: THE CRISIS RESPONSE

THE properness of most people's reactions to a sudden emergency has always fascinated me. Generally we get done what has to be done; *then* we collapse: baby takes a couple of swigs from the Lestoil bottle, mother sticks her fingers down its throat, baby pukes, the problem is resolved. *Then* mother gets the blind willies.

There is some kind of mechanism in us that lies "doggo" until a real threat to survival appears and that then rises to deal with the problem. In medical terms, it's an adrenalin surge: the instant production of a hormone that empowers muscle tissue to contract. It enables a mother to lift the rear end of her car off a pinned child—a feat she could not perform under ordinary circumstances. It enabled the caveman to run faster than the pursuing saber-toothed tiger. The physiologists cannot explain how an adrenalin rush makes the brain work better, but that it does is unarguable. We think properly, instantly, and we act appropriately. For example, I was driving along a rural highway in North Carolina some years ago, in a light rain, when a car, entering from a side road, stalled just as it got onto the pike. I didn't have enough room to stop, and instead of attempting to, I put my car into a broadside skid, fishtailed around the other car, put mine into the opposite slide, and continued on my way. During those few moments I had no thoughts other than those related to avoiding a crash. Four hours later, when I arrived at my house, I started shaking so badly that it took me several minutes to get the key into the door lock.

I was walking along an outside header on an office tower in New York once when I tripped on a tiny projection and hurtled forward. Over my shoulders I carried several coils of wire rope, a weight of perhaps sixty pounds. I couldn't stop myself and was committed to running along the beam—forty-two stories up. While running I thought, how do I stop? I shucked off the coils, not caring where they landed, and as I neared the corner of the building, I flung myself at the column splice—a pair of steel plates no more than eight inches high. I was pretty well cut up, but I didn't go over the side. The men on the plank floor below me who had seen my little act applauded, and I stood up and bowed to them in acknowledgment. Then I sent the punk down to retrieve the coils and went back to work. But when the day was over I had a hell of a case of the shakes.

And there was Charlie Zikas's reaction to a thing which happened to him on a job outside of Bridgeport, Connecticut. It was a tiny building, only four floors high. We were laying on decking. Decking is corrugated sheet iron. It's light; a piece of "Q" deck twenty-four feet by four feet might weigh eighty pounds. It is placed across the beams and headers to form a bottom for the concrete floor that is to be poured upon it. It was a windy day, and Charlie and I were having a tough time keeping the pieces in place; if we let a corner of one get into the wind, the whole thing tried to go over the side. Things were going all right—the welder was right behind us, tacking the sheets down almost as soon as we laid them—when a sudden gust of wind got beneath a sheet that Charlie was laying on the outer edge of the building. The sheet whipped over the side, and so did Charlie. He was right in its middle, and wrapped his arms and feet around it. They hit the ground with a hell of a noise, but Charlie was unhurt. When I talked to him about it, he said he'd had a great deal of time to think: about how pieces of paper seem to slip and slide as they fall to earth. He thought that if he could stay attached to the sheet something like that might happen to him, and that he might then not hit so hard. He was right. He was just shaken up, not seriously hurt. The decking took a beating though.

What made him think to hang on to the sheet metal? Even Charlie doesn't know. . . .

The connector has laid out the bolts for a future piece and now must be careful not to step on them.

# ON SAFETY: COURAGE AND FOOLHARDINESS ARE VERY DIFFERENT THINGS

CROSSING the street, smoking a cigarette, driving a car—all are gambles, as is everything we do. But since the construction worker's life is unusually hazardous, it behooves him to try to better the odds in as many ways as he can.

An ironworker does not wear pants with cuffs, nor shoes with separate heels or steel-reinforced toes, nor inflammable synthetics. If he were to wear cuffed pants, hot slag from a welding or burning operation might catch in them. The same is true of flammable clothing: oxyacetylene torches throw a lot of red-hot cinders a pretty fair distance, and on any large job there are usually several in use at any given moment. The same caution applies to hooded sweatshirts; when the hood is pushed away from the head, the worker is walking around

A tagline man steering a piece as it goes up.

carrying a bucket on his back. There are some terrible stories of men who danced themselves off bridges when tossed rivets accidentally landed in such hoods. Steel-toed shoes are no-no's because if a heavy beam lands on a man's foot it will collapse the strongest shoe and thereby trap the foot within the boot. Better to crush the foot than to pin it within an unremovable case. Separate heels are to be avoided to lessen the danger of tripping over small projections in the iron.

Many ironworkers hate to wear their hard hats, especially in summer, when the itch from the vinyl sweatbands can be very annoying. Raising-gang members, particularly, complain about having to wear them, reasoning that, as they are working above everybody else on the job, who's to drop something on them? Actually the hats do help, even up on top. More than once I've had careless bullwheel operators swing the boom around so that when I straightened up from wrapping a choker around a piece to be lifted, I've banged my head into the waiting hook. With a hat on it's more funny than serious; without one you find out that steel is indeed a great deal harder than flesh and bone. The hooker-on in my first raising gang, working in a great hurry, jumped up from a piece into the hook, fracturing his skull.

If a gang is working several floors below the derrick, their hats stay on even during coffee breaks. The working floor is always covered with discarded bolts, washers, pieces of scrap steel, loose welding rods, and the like. Planks warp and sag with the weight and movement of men and materials, and these things are forever falling through the gaps thus created. There are also showers of sparks from torches being used by men whose coffee breaks don't match yours. Little holes burned into your sweatshirt or jacket are annoying, but not nearly as annoying as little holes burned into your scalp.

Heavy leather gloves are a must. They are also a major expense, especially for the connectors (sliding down columns with them), who may wear out two or three pairs in a week—at five bucks or more per pair. Some connectors do wear fabric gloves, maintaining that they thereby get a better feel of the bolts they install, but most of us don't like the puncture wounds from the beards (frayed or unraveled ends) of the wire rope chokers. A man working with fabric gloves can wear out two pairs a day, so, while they cost only about a third as much per pair, the end expense is about the same.

Properly dressed, the construction worker must also be properly tooled. He'll buy the very best wrenches, beaters, and bars he can afford, file identifying marks on them or paint a part of each in "his" color, and guard them jealously. He will willingly lend, but he does not care to be robbed. And if he catches a thief, he does not bother with a court of law.

Two more areas of safety consciousness remain: *how* the job is run, and *what* is used to run it. If a job—whether a tower, bridge, antenna, or whatever—isn't skillfully managed by the top bosses, the men will quit. Improper management can result in steel being delivered before time, clogging up the work areas. Failure to meet the safety regulations can result in the union steward closing down the job. Failure to get enough material to the site to keep the hands busy can result in boredom, and bored men get careless and make mistakes.

By "what is used to run it," I mean the company equipment: cranes, derricks, trucks, welding machines, torches, bolt-up guns. Defective equipment can kill. A little further on we'll come to a story about a derrick that failed, not killing anyone, but making a bigger mess than most bombs.

A company that doesn't keep its gear in top shape soon acquires a reputation and, when there is plenty of work to go around, has a hard time keeping good men. Nobody wants accidents.

In addition to dressing properly, working hard without showing off *too* much, and staying away from jobs that are run by jerks or that use marginal equipment, there is one more thing that many of us are known to do from time to time—after a two-pound bolt or a wrench has fallen five hundred feet and landed just a couple of inches from us: pray. It can't hurt.

Climbing the column to await the next piece.

# TWO MORE SAFETY TIPS, OR PUTTING ON THE DOGS

PATRICK and I were having coffee on the ground one day, on a job we were doing in New York that was then up some thirty floors. Generally we'd have had our coffee on top, but we'd come down to unload a truck and were just finishing when the punk passed by on his way back from the deli. We took our cups from him and sprawled on the sidewalk. Passers-by often do a sort of yo-yo number when they see ironworkers on the street. With tool belts full of long-pointed wrenches and D-rings and connecting bars and four-pound beaters, we look a little different from other construction workers. They stare at us, then up at the top of the building, then back at us. This morning a plump, fussy-looking man in a Brooks Brothers suit did just that; then, after a moment's hesitation, he spoke to us. "How in God's

Coffee break.

name do you fellows walk around on that stuff? Aren't you afraid of falling?"

"Couldn't fall if I wanted to," Patrick replied. "You see these laces?" He pointed to the top of one of his boots and began unlacing it. Patrick's laces were much longer than they needed to be, and he was in the habit of wrapping their ends three or four times around his boot tops before tying them. He held the now-unwrapped leather thongs apart so that the man could see how long they were. "I tie them together around the bottoms of the beams. That way the worst that can happen if I slip is that I could wind up hanging upside down."

"Good Lord," said the man. "Are those little things *strong* enough?"

"Oh, yes," said Patrick. "It's yak leather."

When he asked if we *all* tied our boots to the beams I said, "No, I and several others wear magnetic shoes." After reflecting briefly on that he got huffy and stamped off.

# IF YOU GOTTA GET HURT IT'S NICE TO HAVE A LOYAL PARTNER

IRONWORKERS generally work in pairs. *All* connectors work in pairs, obviously, since a man is needed at each end of a beam to shove it into place. Each connector is to a great extent responsible for the safety of the other, because if at any given moment one man pushed the piece away from him, the other man would go in the hole or over the side. Naturally, then, connectors who find they make a good team try to remain partners as they move from job to job.

I have a friend who refused to work unless he could connect, and he refused to connect unless his regular partner could work with him. Despite these stipulations they were seldom out of work; they were known as a crackerjack team. "Dick and Rick don't miss a trick!" they'd announce upon arriving at a new job, and they repeated the line every time they solved some particularly difficult connection. But the time finally came, several years ago, when Dick made a careless mistake all on his own and took a hell of a flop, going five floors through open iron, banging into a bunch of stuff on his way down.

The human body is an amazing thing. You see photographs in the papers of cars that look like they've been run over by freight trains and then read that the occupants survived, and you also see pictures of cars that look only slightly damaged and read that the passengers were killed. It's the same with falls from the iron: one man will take a giant tumble and live through it; the next will die from a two-story drop. I know of a man who fell one floor—eleven feet—and has been paralyzed ever since. Yet two elevator installers, working on the twenty-eighth floor of a tower in Chicago, tumbled down a shaft in the center of which was hanging a single cable that they were able to grab —one after falling twenty-three floors, the other after a fall of twenty-six floors. True, they pulled their arms from their sockets and tore the skin and most of the flesh from their hands, but they survived.

When the other men got to Dick they found him alive and conscious. Pretty severely smashed up, but alive. One leg was clearly fractured in at least two places above the knee and one place below it. The injured man grabbed his partner by the forearm and made him swear that under no circumstances would he allow the doctors to take his leg off. At the hospital the doctors did indeed say that the leg had to be amputated, and Rick, still wearing his tool belt, took out his connecting bar and began waving it at the staff. His partner, he said,

---

The tagline brings a piece within the connector's reach.

would rather die than have just one leg, he'd promised Dick that he'd see to it that the leg was not taken off, and he'd decapitate everybody involved in such a procedure. The surgeon explained that the leg was ruined, that there was no way it could be made functional, that there was so much neural damage that even if by some miracle the bones could be gotten together again, the patient would never be able to walk on it, that there existed major danger from infection. . . .

"The poor bastard's worked with his body all his life, Doc," said Rick. "He's got no education; all he knows is construction. You take off his leg he'll shrink up and die anyway, so you might as well give it a shot."

The surgeon bit his lip and went into the operatory, and while Rick stalked around the anteroom in full battle gear—tool belt, hard hat, and his connecting bar gripped tightly in his still-gloved hand— the doctor pinned Dick's leg together. Today Dick walks with a limp, but he walks. He walks on the ground as a supervisor, but he works.

# WHO THE HELL'S IN THE DRIVER'S SEAT, ANYWAY?

W H E N an ironworker is killed or hurt through his own carelessness or stupidity, his fellows are saddened but do not feel personally threatened or frightened. Every ironworker has faith in himself and believes himself neither careless nor stupid. However, when injury results from the failure of a piece of equipment the initial emotion is outrage, followed by a brief surge of fear. Inspections take place at regular intervals throughout the erection of all structures, and there is no legitimate reason for any equipment to prove faulty. But it does happen.

The most spectacular example within my ken was the collapse of a derrick being used to erect a bank on Second Avenue, in New York. It was a middle-sized derrick, with a mast about fourteen stories high

and a boom of about thirteen. The raising gang was taking a load from the street, a heavy load for that size derrick (twenty-one tons), but well within the equipment's capacity. However, as the load was beginning its swing in toward the working floor—the derrick was standing on twenty-three—the bullwheel operator felt a peculiar shudder. He yelled at the gang that something was bad wrong and jumped from his seat. Everybody fled in all directions, not knowing exactly what was going to happen, nor where to look for safety. The derrick began tipping forward at increasing speed as the guy cables, one right after another, parted. All seven of these very heavy wire ropes began whipping every which way, knocking over three of the columns that had already been stood up. They were bolted, of course, to their base plates, and safe enough under ordinary circumstances, but they were not yet connected to any horizontal iron, and could not resist the lateral stress of the cables that were suddenly tangled around them.

The whole rig went into the street: twenty-one tons of load, attached to a hundred and forty feet of boom, attached to a hundred and fifty feet of mast, trailing several tons of attached cables. Two of the three columns that had been knocked over merely banged flat onto the floor beams, splintering the plank floor and making some nice dents in the beams—they weighed seven tons apiece. But the third column found its way into a hole between the beams and plummeted inside the building all the way to the basement, tearing up a lot of steel and concrete on its way down.

*(opposite)* **While three derricks work above the plank floor, a fourth (far right) reaches down over the side for still more iron.** *(overleaf)* **Securing a line on the derrick boom.**

· **57** ·

When a solid material falls a couple of hundred feet it picks up a lot of speed. When it weighs thirty-five or forty tons it picks up a lot of force. When the whole shebang landed, it crashed right through the street and into a forty-eight-inch water main three feet beneath it. By the time the guys in the raising gang got up from their various hastily chosen hiding places to look over the side, what they saw was Second Avenue under two feet of water.

No one was killed. At the moment the rig went over the side the light at the intersection was red, and there were no cars in the block. For some unknowable reason neither were there any pedestrians, though the sidewalks in that area are commonly full of people. Despite all the flying cables and falling columns, no one was struck. There were perhaps two hundred workmen from other trades doing their jobs on the lower floors through which the falling column passed, but no one was hit. That no life was lost was—and still is—widely regarded as a miracle.

Now, what caused the thing to go into the street? Initially the raising gang was accused of having tried to make too heavy a pick, but when the load was gathered up and weighed it was found to be well within acceptable limits. Then the engine operator was accused of having jerked the load (jerking increases apparent weight, as you know if you've ever lost a fish on light line). The culprit turned out to be a turnbuckle: a four-foot-long, forty-pound turnbuckle that secured the cable directly opposite the load. It had had a "fatigue" crack in it (metals subjected to vibration eventually wear out) that had, under the stress of a normally safe pick, sundered. When that first cable let go the others were unable to take the additional strain, and although sound, they, too, parted.

It should never have happened. Every part of a derrick is inspected regularly. Still, it was an almost microscopic crack in a device normally regarded as perfectly reliable: a condition that could easily be missed by even the most conscientious of inspectors.

Nevertheless it *was* defective; it *did* let go; the rig *did* go into the street; and Large George Bullock, who was bounced several feet in the air when one of the falling columns came down within a few inches of his body, took a month off to go fishing in the Everglades.

# CHANGES: WHATCHA GONNA DO WHEN THE WELL RUNS DRY?

FOR a while after the big recession of '72 hit New York, I was able to get work with a little outfit that specialized in removing outdated pipelines in various refineries. We did jobs along the Jersey side of the Hudson and cut up several thousand feet of pipe at a plant in Albany. It was a hairy job, as there was still gasoline vapor in much of the pipe which had a tendency to blow up. Ironworkers all over the Northeast found themselves in serious trouble. Many had bought homes during the golden years of the late sixties, and now had difficulty meeting heavy mortgage payments. They took to bartending or driving cabs, or whatever kind of work they could find. In about a year my little outfit folded, and I was in trouble, too. I found other work for a time, but eventually realized that I was going to have to "boom."

Steering a load to its place on the plank floor.

A boomer is an ironworker who travels from his home local to seek work elsewhere. Those who boom by choice are usually younger men without families, out to see the country or even the world. Fathers and homeowners, however, who cannot afford to be long out of work, boom when forced to by the imbalances inherent in the construction industry. (The country is so large that almost never is the entire industry all sick, or well, at the same time.)

The ironworker's union membership has a dual character: he belongs both to the cell of his local area and to the organism of the international. While that membership entitles him to work anywhere, he still may not ask for any given job until all the local hands have refused it. Thus the boomer's lot, whether he is on the road by choice or necessity, is often not an easy one.

# BOOMING: TO A STRANGE PLACE IN THE DESERT

LARRY and I had been sitting in the hiring hall in Bloomington, California, every morning for two weeks, watching the locals eat up all the jobs that were called out, when the clerk announced openings for "two connectors for Trona." Nobody moved. There were fifteen or twenty men waiting for jobs, yet none answered the call. "What's the matter with the job?" I asked one of them.

"Nothing," he said. "Just that it's the armpit of the world and too far away to get home at night and the people up there are all crazy."

"Any of that bother you?" I asked Larry. He said no, so we bid for and were given the jobs, to start Monday.

As boomers we had no home to go to, anyway. In fact it was much to our advantage to have jobs far away from the hall: travel and subsistance monies are scaled to distance, and Trona was so far away (over a hundred miles) that the extra money amounted to twenty dollars a day, yet *our* expenses, since we were living in a motel already, would be no greater. Maybe less, we thought, happily; the desert wasn't likely to be a high-rent district.

At supper that night with Denny and Joe, two men who had worked at Trona, we got a little more dope. What we were being sent to was a huge chemical plant, to work on a $300 million expansion. It is there because the desert floor is nine hundred feet deep in soda ash (from which fertilizers and such products as Borax are made). Apart from the processing of this resource, there is no other reason on earth for anyone ever to be anywhere *near* the area.

The town of Trona exists simply to service the plant workers. It is a lonely place *in* a lonely place. West of Trona the first town is Ridgecrest, twenty-five miles distant and not a hell of a lot bigger nor appreciably more attractive; to the east it is sixty-eight miles to the nearest gas station, at the entrance to Death Valley; one cannot go north nor directly south: there are no roads at all.

Trona is not exactly a metropolis. It does have a clinic, a pharmacy, a couple of general shops, two places to eat and one in which to drink, a bank, a grocery, a gas station, two churches, a movie house open three nights a week, and an iron-barred, one-room blockhouse in which those who fail to obey the town's only stop sign may be invited to spend the night. There is a trailer camp just west of town, and just beyond is a rock on which someone has written in spray paint, "This is not hell, but you can see it from here."

"You're lucky," Denny said, "to be going up there in November. When Joe and I were there it was *hot*."

"How hot," said Larry, because one of us had to ask, "was it?" This set Denny and Joe to telling stories—of iron that expanded so much in the midday sun and shrank so much in the cool desert night that heavily bolted joints sometimes sheared right off, and of men who collapsed with heat prostration or who drank so much water that they began to vomit uncontrollably and finally had to be treated for dehydration.

Most of their anecdotes were moderately interesting examples of men working under extreme conditions; one was bizarre.

"The connectors," Joe said, "all carried burlap sacks folded up into butt-sized pads. When they had to sit down on the iron to bolt up a connection they slipped these beneath them. Without something like that there was just no way you could sit down. One day one of the guys got the bright idea of wetting down his sack. He climbed down to the water cooler and soaked the pad, and then with this big stupid grin on his face went back to his connection and sat down. Pretty soon he was squirming, but he still had a couple bolts to make, so he had to stay there. It wasn't too much longer before you could see steam rising from his pants." At this, Larry groaned. "Take it or leave it, whichever you like," Joe said, shrugging, "but that's what happened. Anybody who was there in the summer can tell you that any time you wanted to see steam all you had to do was spit on any piece of iron. . . . Anyhow, by the time he'd got the last bolt stuck and tightened, the guy was *really* squirming. He jumped to his feet, shucked his tool belt the fastest way he could, and came scooting down the nearest column. By the time he got to the water cooler he'd got his buttons loose and his pants were down around his knees. Another man tipped the whole cooler over on the guy's butt, but the damage was already done. He was fried—second degree burns. They took him to the clinic and from there, I guess, to the hospital. I never saw him again."

Neither Larry nor I took this story seriously, but a week later, after we'd been at Trona long enough to have made some acquaintances, some of whom had been there in the summer, I repeated Joe's story, skeptically, at coffee break.

"You'd *better* believe it," one of them said.

"Yeah?" I replied.

"Second and *third* degree burns," he growled, dropping his pants and bending over. A good portion of his behind was scar tissue.

"Was hot here, in the summer," said someone in the back.

Larry and I kept silent.

At three o'clock Monday morning we started off from Riverside for the job. The route took us through San Bernadino, up a steep climb to Cajon Pass, then gradually down the eastern slope of the mountains, and out onto the plains of the high desert. We had figured, since the map showed the road to be a two-lane highway that led nowhere unless you followed it all the way to Las Vegas, that we'd have the night all to ourselves. For the first two hours we did. There was no

At work around one of the chokers of a derrick guy.

traffic at all, and the miles rolled darkly by. Then headlights appeared behind us, soon followed by another pair, and not long afterward by a third. A little later Larry mumbled, "Can't be gamblers; there's too many of 'em." He jerked his thumb toward the rear, and I looked around. Behind us were dozens of pairs of lights, strung all the way down the perfectly straight road to the faintest night horizon.

"You don't suppose they're all going to Trona?" I wondered.

"Where else is there to go?" he answered. Just then the guy who'd been tailgating us shot past, and as he swung back into the right-hand lane our lights lit up a sticker on his bumper that read, "Where the hell's Trona?" The gap he left behind us was immediately filled, and it wasn't long before *that* car passed us, at a blind rise, without the least hesitation and at impressive speed. There was a similar sticker on his bumper, though we barely had time to read it.

"You know what it is?" said Larry. "It's the Trona Snake. And these crazy bastards who pass on hills at a hundred and twenty miles an hour are our co-workers."

Apparently nobody wanted to get to Trona any earlier than he had to, and all had waited until the last possible minute before leaving home. Now in the false dawn, they were going hell-for-leather north, and God help anybody who happened to be heading south.

But there was no southbound traffic at all. We soon learned that everybody in that part of the state was aware of the Monday return of the swarm to the hive and the Friday exodus, and the locals made it a point never to travel in the opposite direction.

For the last few miles before the road reaches Trona it snakes through a low ridge and down a kind of ragged scarf. We turned the last bend and the top of the valley lay suddenly visible in the early light. At the northern end sprawled the plant. White smoke rose from a dozen scattered tall stacks, black smoke from several others. There was no wind, and the smoke simply hung over the valley like a veil. One of the plants was a properly rectangular building with a huge annex in the form of a monstrous steel-sheeted A-frame chalet, but most of the place looked like the world's largest erector set: a collection of girders framing huge boilers and cookers and furnaces and driers and sifters and eighty-foot-high retorts. The sun wasn't yet up, and from the dark silhouettes of the towers and buildings thousands of tiny white lights winked at us. Those lights, so small, illuminating only a few square feet of catwalk grating or a tiny patch of stack or a short run of steel stairs, served simply to exaggerate the already powerful sense of isolation. The whole complex—the stark plant and the scruffy village that leaned against it—squatted like some kind of lost creature that had given up trying to find its way home and was instead trying to scratch out a nest for itself in the unyielding ground. The desert encroached upon it everywhere. Mesquite and sage grew to the very edge of man's contrivances; tumbleweed rolled along the town's few streets and jammed under the frames of the vehicles in the company parking lots; sand found its way into everything.

"That," said Larry, shaking his head, "is the ugliest sight I've ever seen."

# WHERE THERE'S SMOKE THERE'S FIRE, AND IT DOESN'T TAKE A WHOLE LOT, EITHER

MELVIN was a "mungo master." "Mungo" is salable metal scrap —the cutoff ends of copper or brass tubing and the like. Technically such pieces remain the property of the contractor who brought the material to the job in the first place, but there are a number of construction workers who are adept at "liberating" such scraps via their duffel bags at week's end. This may sound like small potatoes, and I suppose in corporate terms it is, but even little things mount up. The winter that Melvin and I worked together in Manhattan, copper was bringing over a dollar a pound; Melvin, who could spot a two-inch piece of small pipe at thirty feet, regularly carted home such quantities of metal that the veins on his neck stood out as he pretended to be leaving the site with nothing more than four or five pounds of his own dirty coveralls: "nonchalanting it," as Yogi Berra once said about a difficult fly ball.

One Friday afternoon that February it rained and sleeted, and all the ironworkers were sent home except Melvin and me as we were working on some detail stuff on lower floors. On one of our numerous trips between floors Melvin discovered that someone had left a practically brand-new welding lead on one of the staircases. A welding lead is a length of rubber-insulated, twisted copper cable, about an inch in diameter, and it is very heavy, perhaps a pound a foot. The section that Melvin came across was about a hundred feet long, and he had no sooner begun dragging it across the floor than he was cursing with the effort. (Its bottom end lay some nine floors beneath us.)

"What the hell are you doing now?" I asked, annoyed because I suspected I was going somehow to become involved in another of his petty thefts.

"See that salamander?" he returned. I nodded. A salamander is a fifty-five gallon drum on little legs. It is filled with coke and lit with a torch. Coke burns like charcoal—virtually without flame or smoke and quite slowly. One filling will keep a drum alive all day. There were more than a dozen on the floor, their purpose being to provide just enough heat to enable the newly poured concrete on the floor above to cure properly. "I'm gonna cook the insulation off this cable so's I don't have to carry all the extra weight." More mungo, I saw, and not scrap, either.

"You gotta be kidding," I said, shaking my head. "You know what rubber does when you burn it?"

"What's a little smoke?" he countered. I shrugged and went back to work. Mere common sense was never a deterrent to Melvin's thirst for mungo.

For the next twenty minutes, accompanied by some mighty cursing, Melvin labored at getting the whole nine-story length of cable up the stairs and over to the salamander, where he coiled as much of it as would fit into the top of the drum. The first smoke to appear was gray and wispy, and I thought for a moment that he might somehow get away with it. But as the fire began to take hold, the smoke turned black and the blustery wind carried it over the side of the building. While Melvin poked at the fire with a three-foot-long two-by-four, hacking and coughing and looking for all the world like one of the witches in *Macbeth* stirring her cauldron, I ran to the edge of the floor. Torrents of smoke were now spilling over the side, and people were already looking up and pointing. From thirty floors above them I couldn't hear what was being said, but the message was clear: there was going to be trouble. I ran back to the salamander—which in all the smoke I might not have been able to find had it not been for the noise of Melvin's coughing—and shouted, "Damn it all to hell, Melvin, get that stuff outta there. In a minute we're going to have the fire department up here!" And even as Melvin opened his mouth I heard the first of the sirens below. The New York City Fire Department is a *very* quick outfit.

"It ain't cooked yet," said Melvin, whom I could no longer see at all. I called him something choice and ran back to the edge, and saw

Waiting for the other end to be made up before sliding a knife connection in.

that there were numbers of fire trucks in the street and numbers of firemen grabbing axes and Halloran tools from their racks, running into the building. I sped back to the salamander and told Melvin the firemen were on their way. Out of the smoke came his disembodied voice saying firmly, "I told youse, it ain't cooked yet." I swore at him again. "T'ey can't tell from down there exactly where it is," he said. "Go stand by t'e elevator and if t'ey try to get off here tell 'em it's four, five floors higher."

"You're nuts," I coughed back at him. "That's obstructing justice, or something."

"Just go do it, will youse? Like I said, it ain't cooked yet." So, recognizing that I was just as nuts as Melvin, I went to stand at the elevator. Pretty soon I could hear men shouting and the sounds of the elevator stopping at lower floors. When the car arrived at our floor, I pointed upward and said, "I think it's four floors higher."

"Thanks," said a man in a white hat, and off they went. A moment later they were back. Before they got quite to our level I shouted into the shaftway, "Fella just told me it's two floors down!" and off they tore again.

When next they returned they practically knocked me over spilling out, and as he brushed past me the man in the white helmet said, "What the hell are you trying to do, buster?"

"Aw, there *ain't* any damned fire," I answered. Then one of the men who had rounded the corner toward the salamander called out, "My God, look at the smoke!" and the whole crew advanced upon it. I strolled along behind them, thinking that I would probably be better advised to go in some other direction, but curious to see what would happen next.

Black as it still was, the smoke had by now abated somewhat, and I could dimly make out the silhouette of Melvin at his cauldron, in a batter's stance with his two-by-four, shaking its glowing end at the approaching firefighters. "Get away!" he kept shouting. "It ain't cooked yet!"

"What in God's name is he doing?" wondered the man in the white hat.

"Just cooking something," I said, from a safe distance to the rear.

"Put it out!" commanded White Hat, and his men resumed their advance upon Melvin, who kept screaming that it wasn't a fire, it was only rubber, and it wasn't cooked yet. "Put it out!" White Hat repeated.

"Come any closer and I'll deck youse," shouted Melvin, wagging his bat, and the lead fireman came to a halt. His axe was still poised, but his feet weren't moving. Melvin seemed to feel that he'd gained a slight edge, for there was a slight tone of superiority in his voice when he spoke again. "T'at's fine," he growled, "just fine. Youse just stay put."

But Melvin's hopes for a standoff were short-lived, for right then, from off to leeward where the smoke was thickest, came another fireman at full tilt. With a move worthy of an NFL blocking back, he

*(overleaf)* Signaling the derrick to come down a little so that the connectors can align the holes.

got a shoulder into Melvin's side and knocked him clear out of the ball game: his two-by-four flew into the air, he disappeared into the far smoke, and by the time he'd picked himself up and returned to the scene there wasn't anything to return to. The firemen had knocked the salamander over, raked its contents out upon the floor, and sprayed the whole mess with white froth from their extinguishers. While they were doing this White Hat came over to me and said, "Who *are* you guys, anyway?"

"Just of couple of wire lathers," I answered. "We were just up here tying down some loose rods to try to make the rainy day when Freddy found this old beatup welding lead and decided to cook it down for the copper. He didn't mean no harm."

"He didn't, huh?" snorted White Hat.

"Well, no, sir," I replied. "We didn't know it smoked like that."

"You didn't, huh?" White Hat sneered. I hung my head and wagged it slowly. I'll bet you're a brilliant conversationalist at the dinner table, I thought to myself, but I knew better than to say it aloud. "I'll need your names," White Hat announced, drawing a small pad from his pocket.

"The guy that your man took out," I said," is Freddy Corcoran, and I'm Charley Lindbergh." White Hat cocked an eye and fixed me with a disbelieving scowl. Melvin was standing a few feet away, rubbing his side but saying nothing. I sighed and lowered my head briefly. "It's given me trouble all my life," I said. "My father's last name really is Lindbergh, and he's an aviation nut and even my middle initial is *M.* It ain't easy." This seemed to satisfy White Hat, and after making a few more notes he closed his pad, announced that a man would come by the job Monday to take a full report, gathered his men, and left.

When they were gone Melvin said, "Youse is pretty quick wit' t'e words."

"I was counting on his not recognizing Corcoran's name," I answered.

"Who is Corcoran?"

"He was an early pilot, too." Melvin snickered, but then began poking morosely at his half-cooked cable. It looked pretty gummy and was caked with white powder and it smelled like hell. Melvin sniffed at it and wrinkled his nose.

"Rubber stinks," he said. "Let's go home."

That was the only time I've ever known Melvin to give up on a piece of mungo.

# WHERE DO WE GO FROM HERE?

UP TO NOW, ironworkers have been the builders of the tallest and largest structures in the world. It will not always be so. It has been true since steel was developed around the turn of the century. Steel! Malleable, ductile, weldable, cutable. . . . With it engineers were able to design and ironworkers to build by 1912 the Woolworth Tower, which was 765 feet high; in 1930 the Chrysler Tower was completed, standing 1046 feet; less than a year later the queen of the classic skyscrapers was up—the Empire State Building, 102 stories, 1244 feet, $11\frac{1}{2}$ inches from the street to the top of its light. And now there are the World Trade Center twin towers, 110 stories, 1350 feet high, and the Sears Tower in Chicago, the tallest building in the world, with the same number of stories as the Trade Center, but because of slightly higher ceilings, about a hundred feet higher.

An outside header goes into place.

Yet, any ironworker must feel a chill in his spine when he sees such sights as the seventy-two-story hotel recently completed in Atlanta: except for the few lowest floors, it is built of reinforced concrete that contains no structural steel at all. Ironworkers are not allowed to work with any material but their own. Many new buildings are being made of reinforced concrete, but to date that hotel is by far the largest.

And there will be other materials—new alloys, anodized aluminum, perhaps—possibly even plastics . . . There have been more changes in construction materials in the last ten years than in all the thirty-eight years between the completion of the Empire State and my own entry into the trade in 1968.

We are dinosaurs, lumbering along in an increasingly arid world, and are well-advised to urge our children to acquire skills beyond our own. Physical courage, agility, and pride will always be needed by the men who build skyscrapers and bridges and radiotelescope antennas, but the mechanical techniques are changing, and we must adapt or perish.

# EPILOGUE

WHILE it exists, though, it's a young man's trade. At least, connecting is. Most connectors move into less-demanding roles by the time they turn thirty. *All* ironwork is physically demanding, but connecting is supremely so: clambering up and sliding down tall columns eight hours a day while wearing fifty or more pounds of equipment, swinging sixteen-pound mauls (with one hand while hanging on with the other) to beat heavy beams into place, levering (with bars a mere two feet long) recalcitrant five- and six-ton headers into alignment between quite rigid ten- or twelve-ton columns. Yes, connecting is a young man's job. I don't do it anymore. I was thirty-five when I first got into the trade, thirty-six when I first went connecting, forty-four when I finished my last job. Long enough.

At the end I was working in California. When I came back East a friend said, "How can you give up a trade that pays nearly fourteen dollars an hour?" I replied that it didn't really add up to all that much. Yes, the hourly rate was good, but the wasted time between jobs was not, that the construction industry is particularly responsive to recessions and during such times, fourteen times nothing is still nothing, that the ego trip ("My God, do you guys *really* walk around up there?") had long since paled, and that the old body had decided it was tired of hurting.

It was fun while it lasted.